Discovering
CARTS AND WAGONS

John Vince

Drawings by David Wray

Shire Publications Ltd

CONTENTS

ACKNOWLEDGEMENTS: The author is pleased to acknowledge the assistance he has received from the following: The David Wray Collection: an unpublished library of detailed measured drawings of all types of farm vehicles and implements—made during a period of twenty-five years continuous research.
Dr. Levi Fox, O.B.E., D.L.; E. W. Aubrook, F.M.A.; Anthea V. Diver, B.A.; J. Geraint Jenkins, Esq.; Mrs. D. J. Bullard; B. Loughbrough, Esq., M.A.; Athon W. Gill, Esq.; C. A. Jewell, Esq., B.Sc.; Rev. Ronald Appleton; F. C. Thompson, Esq.; David C. Young, Esq.; Bryan P. Blake, A.M.A.; Ted and Christine Endres; Robert Patience, Esq.; Michael Keefe, Esq.; The Shakespeare Birthplace Trust; Oxford City and County Museum; Wye College, University of London; City of Norwich Museums; The University of Reading—Museum of English Rural Life; The County Councils of Staffordshire, Worcestershire, Hampshire and Rutland; The County Borough of Brighton; The National Trust; City Museum, Bristol; The Tolson Memorial Museum, Huddersfield.

INTRODUCTION

In the days before internal combustion engines the horse provided a large part of man's motive power. A century ago England's highways and byeways echoed with the creak of the horse and cart. Even small villages had a carter who made his way into the outside world once or twice a week to bring back essential supplies that the village community could not produce for itself. The horse-drawn world of Queen Victoria's reign has passed but many of the vehicles built then have endured and they may be found in museums, under hedgerows or in barns. Farm carts and wagons were made to last and some of those preserved today are surprisingly old. Today these vehicles have become collectors' items and in the pages which follow their structural features are described and some of the principal regional variations are explained. Many of the vehicles listed represent the culmination of centuries of tradition, craftsmanship and design.

A world in a hurry had no place for the steady pace of the wagon, and its replacement by an alternative form of transport was inevitable. Even obsolescence, however, cannot rob the best carts and wagons of their natural elegance which is derived from both function and design.

Factory made in Bristol. A harvest cart or Scotch cart used on the Cotswolds and in parts of Oxfordshire.

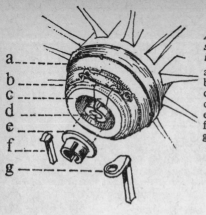

A typical hub, nave or stock and fittings for an iron axle arm.

a Stock bond.
b Stopper clasp.
c Stopper.
d Iron axle arm.
e Collet.
f Lynch pin.
g Special lynch pin sometimes fitted to nearside rear wheel for attaching a roller scotch.

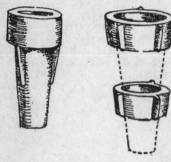

Every stock is lined with an iron sleeve or box. That for an iron axle is in one piece. For the older wooden axles two separate boxes were used, one at the front and one at the back of the stock.

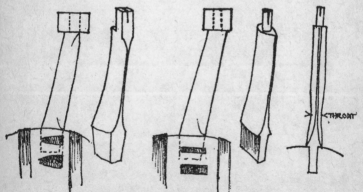

Square tongue spoke used with strakes or hoops.

Round tongue spoke used only with hoops.

WHEELS

The safety and efficiency of both carts and wagons depended upon the construction of the wheel. The spokes radiated from a hub—or nave or stock, to use the wheelwright's terms—made always of elm. The spokes, of oak for its strength, were made with the greatest accuracy before their tenons were ferociously hammered into the deeply mortised nave. This was in turn strengthened by its stock bonds. The outer ends of the spokes were sometimes square tongued—to prevent twisting (see opposite). Latterly a round tongue—like a dowel—was considered adequate. The wheel's rim was composed of several felloes into which the spokes were firmly fixed. Wedges driven into the ends of the spokes also helped to keep them in position. The felloes were often made of ash but beech, oak and elm were acceptable alternatives. A row of strakes or a hoop tyre bound the wheel's parts together.

Dishing

The rim, spokes and nave of a cart or wagon wheel are not constructed in the same plane. This arrangement, which gives wheels a 'dished' appearance, was not arrived at by accident. It had a clear purpose. As a horse moves in the shafts it imparts a slight swaying motion to the vehicle and wheels tend to move in two directions at once—forwards and side to side on the axle arm. If a wheel had its spokes set in the same plane as the rim and the nave this sideways motion would tend to break the wheel apart. The cone-shaped structure of a dished wheel would not succumb to the sideways thrust because its cross section forms a triangle—about the strongest shape known to engineers. Another consideration which favoured the dished shape was the need to keep the upper part of the wheel clear of the vehicle's sides. A wheel made in a single plane would have its upper half too close to the body if the axle arm was horizontal. Axle arms were, however, made with a definite dip downwards (page 7, g) and this allowed the upper half of the wheel to stand clear of the vehicle's sides. A wheel made in a single plane and mounted on a downward sloping axle arm would not, of course, have its spokes vertically opposed to the ground—they would slope inwards and tend to tear themselves out of the nave. Such a wheel would not be able to support a load satisfactorily even when at rest. In contrast a dished wheel, positioned on a sloping axle arm, will present

5

its spokes in turn vertically to the ground. Dished wheels solved all the sideways thrust difficulties, the problem of sufficient distance between the upper edge and the vehicle's sides and the need for weight bearing spokes to be at right angles to the road surface. Although a wheel may look a simple affair it is in fact the craftsman's considered answer to several distinct but related technical problems.

Strakes and hoops

The wooden rim of the wheel—the felloes—is protected with an iron tyre. There are two kinds of tyres. Strake tyres are made in sections and each section overlaps a felloe joint to give it protection. Large nails are used to keep the strakes in place. Wheels with strake tyres always have square tongued spokes. Hoop tyres are fitted to wheels with square or round tongued spokes—see page 4. On wagons around the Severn Basin, Gloucestershire, both kinds of tyres will be found on the same wheel. Hoop tyres were made by the blacksmith so that they were slightly less than the diameter of the wheel. Tyres of this sort had to be fitted to the wheel after they had been heated in the fire. Wheelwrights and blacksmiths alike usually had a tyring place where this work was carried out. The wheel had to be securely bolted down to the ground before the tyre was fixed—otherwise the tremendous forces generated by a cooling tyre could pull a wheel out of shape.

Strakes too were fixed while red hot but they did not bind a wheel together as firmly as the hooped tyre. For this reason square tongues were used in conjunction with strakes to add strength and rigidity to the felloes.

THE CART

Many people confuse carts and wagons. A cart or tumbril is the simplest sort of wheeled vehicle man could ever contrive. It has two wheels mounted on a single axle which takes the weight of the cart body.

Carts were once employed in all parts of the British Isles and archaeologists have shown that carts were in use in the days when the Glastonbury lake village was inhabited in the fourth century B.C. It is rather difficult nowadays for us to appreciate that once every farm had its collection of carts and nearly every village had a carrier who provided a vital link with the outside world. Most farm carts were constructed so that they could be tipped up to quickly discharge a load.

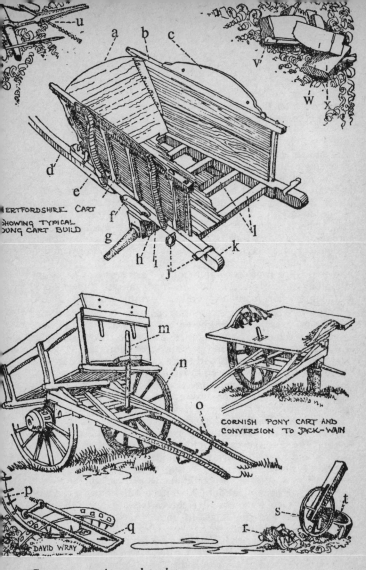

HERTFORDSHIRE CART
SHOWING TYPICAL
DUNG CART BUILD

CORNISH PONY CART AND
CONVERSION TO JACK-WAIN

DAVID WRAY

Cart construction and tools

a. forehead; b. top rave; c. top board; d. shaft; e. strouter; f. dirt board;
g. iron axle arm; h. clip; i. axle or exbed; j. tail ladder irons; k. side or sole;
l. shutters; m. tip stick; n. felloes; o. long staple; p. wheel strakes; q. samson;
r. chalk line; s. traveller (for measuring the internal diameter of tyres); t. axle
box; u. augers; v. hollow plane; w. compass plane; x. moulding plane.

They were used for all kinds of work around the farm. Hay and corn harvest were important parts of the farming year and the carrying capacity of the cart was increased at such times by the addition of harvest ladders at the front and rear. These allowed the load to overhang the cart body. Care had to be taken in the manner of loading and the balance of the cart had to be arranged so that the horse did not have too much weight on its back or below its belly. The size of a cart and its weight was partly determined by the pulling power of a single horse. Only one horse will fit between a pair of shafts. Additional horses were sometimes attached, in a line, in front of the shaft horse, however, if the load was particularly heavy or the going very bad. Harvest work did not require a cart that tipped but there were many different tasks about the farm which made a tipping cart essential. Muck spreading was one task that called for a tip-cart and among the variety of carts that would be in use on a farm of moderate size there would be several muck carts. Tip carts were also useful for root crops and stones. Farmers were not alone in finding tip-carts useful vehicles and various traders—coal merchants, quarrymen and builders—employed them too.

Carts were probably more numerous than the heavy wagons for several reasons. To begin with a cart was a smaller and less costly vehicle. A cart can be worked by a single horse and in terms of horse power carts were more easily drawn than wagons. On a good road surface a horse with a cart had to exert a pull of 51.4 lbs to move a ton. This compared with the 68.1 lbs of effort per ton required to pull a wagon. On arable land the difference was even more striking. The cart horse had to exert a pull of 201 lbs per ton and a two horse wagon needed 295.2 lbs of energy for the same load. In other words a cart needed about 28 per cent less pulling than a wagon. The average cart could carry a load of from 18 to 22 cwts and for most purposes a single horse was an adequate source of power. An old farming manual suggests that a farm of up to 100 acres could be worked adequately with three carts. Farms of about 200 acres needed one wagon and four carts. Two wagons and eight carts were required, however, for 500 acre holdings. In some parts of England, of course, carts were used exclusively. One of the things which helped to determine the kind of vehicle to be used was the nature of the land itself. Very hilly districts with steep or winding lanes did not favour the use of the wagon which required a greater amount of room for turning. Hilly areas could best be served by carts which may have needed to make more visits to a harvest field but could perform more efficiently. In Cornwall, a county noted for its undulating terrain, carts predominated in horse drawn days. Cornish carts were very light affairs and the box-like cart body (page 7) was usually detachable. The same pair of wheels was employed to carry the flat body of the 'wain' which had a very elementary guard that curved over each of the wheels. These wains were used for harvest work, as the greater area of the flat platform allowed the volume of the load to be increased.

Carts with very similar characteristics (see page 3) were built in Bristol during the latter part of the last century. They were used in many parts of the Cotswolds and the South Midlands. These carts were not made to tip. They have very shallow sides and the boarded lades prevent the load from fouling the wheels. Long harvest poles were placed at each corner of the slender body to help give added stability to the tall load. Poles of this kind were used in many parts of England as we shall see later. A species of cart which was employed only for harvest work could once be found in Yorkshire. It had a long body which enabled it to carry a larger load than the conventional dung cart.

Dung cart construction

There are two kinds of cart construction. The dung cart has features which certain other carts do not share. A cart body is really a box on wheels. Any load placed in the cart will tend to push downwards on the floor and outwards on the sides. The floor and the sides must be made strong enough to contain the load, and dung carts—which were often used for very dense burdens—had to be particularly robust. They are called dung carts because that was their principal function but they were used for all manner of other work as well. At hay-time and harvest they were fitted with ladders and helped to bring home the hay and the sheaves.

Heavy loads need to be supported by a stout frame and dung carts have long and heavy sides which are joined together by similarly stout shutters. From the sides rise the standards which are mortised at both ends—into the sides and top rave. The top rave is longer at the rear than the plank sides. At this point a long iron pillar-bolt is fixed which joins the top rave to the side. Each end of the pillar is threaded to take a nut. As the nuts are tightened they cramp the rear end of the cart side in a vice-like grip. There is a very good reason for extra strength at this point. The sides of the cart extend some eighteen inches or so beyond the side planks and this extension protects the rear shutlock from damage when the cart is tipped up and strikes the ground.

9

The underside of each projecting side is protected with a strip of iron. If there was no additional mechanical support the continuous banging of the sides on the ground would slowly shake the mortised standards free and the vertical sides would fall apart. The pillar-bolt secures the side framework against such damage. Extra strength is given to the sides by the fixing of curved strouters which served exactly the same purpose as buttresses on a mediaeval church. There are frequently two strouters to each side bolted at the top through the top rave and at the bottom to the side. The frontboard is firmly fixed to both sideboards.

Two iron brackets at the rear allow a ladder to be attached at harvest time and support the side against the outward thrust of the load.

Most people are impressed by the way in which carts and wagons have their various members shaved into curious and elegant curves. When the painter gets to work these delicate shapes become even more obvious. There is nevertheless a very practical reason for this embellishment—it is not pure decoration even though it may convey that idea at first glance. Dung carts were heavy vehicles and every inessential ounce of timber added to the horse's burden. It was for this reason that the axles, rails, standards and various other members were carefully shaved off and their surplus bulk discarded. More material could be shaved away from the middle of a standard than from its jointed ends. Where one timber met another the maximum strength was needed and nothing was subtracted at all. Exactly the same considerations were involved in wagon design.

The cart floor was an important feature. In dung carts the floorboards were placed so that they ran parallel to the cart sides—in wheelwright's jargon they were long boarded. Once again there is a very practical reason for this arrangement. The task of raking out the contents of a laden cart—even when it was in the tipped-up position—would have been very frustrating if the boards were placed at right angles to the sides. In the nature of things boards will warp and cross boards would have warped to catch the unwary tines of a muck rake. Long boarding was clearly essential in a dung cart and the underframe described above allowed long boards to be nailed directly to the shutters (page 7, 1).

Raved carts

An alternative method of cart body construction made use of summers which run parallel with the sides. Carts constructed in this manner were often cross boarded—the boards

Left: *Typical plank side construction in which one bolt locks together the top rave, the 2" thick deal sideboard, and the main side of the cart or wagon.*

Right: *Another method of building more cheaply. Standards were bolted to the main sides instead of morticed into them. Many traditional builders also used this method in one way or another.*

A plank sided tip cart, sometimes called a Scotch cart.

could be nailed directly to the sides and summers. Cross boarded vehicles were used by tradesmen of various kinds and they also had certain uses on the farm. Carts constructed with summers were also frequently long boarded. If long boards were required additional timbers, called keys, were added. Oak keys were placed at right angles to the summers and were mortised through them. The keys were essential for two reasons—they provided support for the long boards and points for nailing. Long boards rested on the keys and their upper edges were level with the summers. This style of construction is also used on the body of the wagon.

Carts constructed with summers are often less crude than the humble dung cart. Older examples frequently display the refinements and regional characteristics that we find on wagons. Craftsmen-built carts, made in village wheelwrights' shops, followed traditional designs. For this reason we can still find carts with panelled or spindled sides that are divided about half way up by a midrail. Most of the local carts which remain today however—outside museums—cannot claim such traditional origins.

Scotch carts

At quite an early stage in the nineteenth century ideas of mass production began to invade English agriculture. Wheels were made with cast iron hubs. These appeared as early as 1846. Factory-made carts and wagons began to challenge the village craftsman's traditional monopoly and the character of the village wheelwright's work slowly began to change—although it was a very long time before it became virtually extinct. Makers of mass produced vehicles were proud enough of their work to make sure that their names appeared on the cast iron hubs and on the maker's plates that were often fitted to the side of the vehicle. Some prominent names to look for are: 'Tasker, Andover'; 'Woods, Stowmarket'; 'William Croskill, Beverley'; 'E. H. Roberts, Deanshanger'; 'Wilder, Wallingford'; and 'Bristol Waggon Works'. The heavy factory-built carts had plank sides held in place by long bolts that clamped the side and top rave together (page 11). Many village wheelwrights gradually adapted their traditional methods and began to produce vehicles made in the factory manner. At some stage in the nineteenth century carts made in Scotland began to appear in East Anglia. The reasons for this importation of carts into wagon country are not readily obvious. Factory-made carts, from such places as Maybole, Ayrshire—Messrs. Jack and Sons, were given the name 'Scotch carts'. This label came to have a wide currency in the course of time and it was used very loosely to describe a wide variety of different cart designs.

Various writers have mentioned 'Scotch carts' and when this term appears it usually needs to be interpreted with some degree of caution. Freda Derrick's *Country Craftsman* provides a drawing of a 'Scotch cart' which is really a South Midlands harvest cart (page 3). In contrast, so called 'Scotch carts' in Buckinghamshire have a very different look. There they have plank sides, will tip up, often have iron wheel hubs and will be long boarded on shutters. The real Scotch cart will most likely be encountered these days in East Anglia. It will tip, have plank sides, an arched frontboard and provision for harvest ladders at front and rear. The wheels will probably be at least four inches wide and the naves made of elm. This very general description clearly had many variations which depended upon any given cart's provenance. The Scotch cart type was durable, cheap and efficient in operation. All these factors helped to make the style popular and it was eventually reproduced in both factory and village workshops.

Decoration

All carts were painted and the colours used depended upon the local preferences which are described later. The most general colours employed were red for the wheels and blue for the bodywork. One of the most interesting things to note about Scotch carts is the curious style of decoration they brought with them from north of the Border. This characteristic decoration was copied by English painters too and its use has been noted on unquestionably English wagons. The basic idea behind the motif used was a pair of eyes—looking forward to see danger or reflect the gaze of the evil eye. Some forms of this style are called 'spectacles'. Other render-

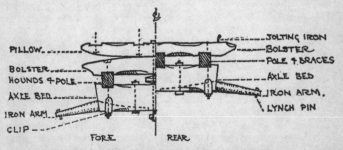

General arrangement of typical undercarriage.

13

ings vary from two isolated circles to more complex patterns that are not unlike a butterfly's wings. The predilection for painting eyes on inanimate objects goes back a long way— the Greeks decorated the bows of their galleys in this manner —and not so long ago certain Spitfires and Hurricanes were similarly embellished. Whatever the origin of the style in the British Isles it is undoubtedly ancient and may have some distant relationship with the traditional paintings to be observed on carts in both Malta and Sicily. Readers who wish to explore this subject further should turn to C. F. Tebbutt's informative article on the subject—"Some Cart and Wagon Decorations of the British Isles and Eire"; *Man* Vol LV, August 1955.

Spring carts

Not all carts were made as robustly as the vehicles that were principally employed on the farm. Village carriers and other tradesmen needed some form of wheeled transport. There is a basic difference between tradesmen's vehicles and the agricultural variety. During the nineteenth century the roads were improved. Lighter carts were introduced and they were fitted with springs to give a smoother ride. Their wheels were still rather large—over 5 feet—but narrower than the wheels of farm carts. Wheels a mere two inches wide needed a fairly good road surface. Spring carts did not have wooden axles but ones made at the blacksmith's forge.

The variety of carts in use at the end of the last century was far too great to record here in detail. Simple box carts with a tail board that dropped down could be used by many kinds of tradesmen—millers, market gardeners, grocers, builders, fish merchants and cheesemakers. Carts were often fitted with a canvas cover, supported on a wooden framework, to give protection in bad weather. Very light forms of the cart were developed and some simply provided seats for passengers.

Some carts were made for special purposes and market carts and horse boxes come into this class. Dairymen too made use of carts designed for their special needs. Milk, carried in a churn, stood at the front of the cart and a low step allowed the milkman to enter from the rear to scoop out each measure of milk for the housewife—waiting with her jug. A popular variation on the milkman's cart was that used by the ice cream vendor—he used the same style of cart but it was decorated and protected by a candy-striped awning held aloft on twisted brass columns. Equally ornate lettering on the cart sides proclaimed the vendor's name.

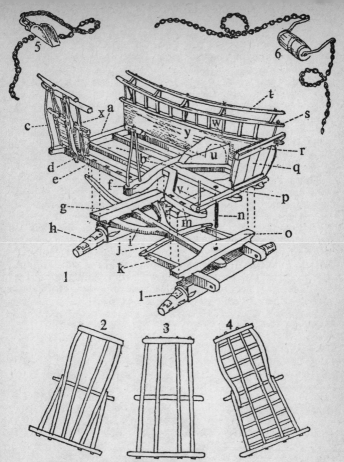

1. **Exploded diagram of a Suffolk wagon.**
   a. shutlock; b. summers; c. hind staff; d. strouter; e. side or sole; f. crossledge; g. bolster; h. axle arm (wood); i. braces; j. sway bar; k. hounds; l. iron wearing plates or clouts; m. front side or crook; n. king pin; o. bolster; p. nosepiece; q. front board; r. forehead; s. top rave; t. outrave; u. locking arch; v. pillow; w. middle rave; x. standards; y. side boards.

2. *Bed construction of Derbyshire and other West Midlands half locking wagons.*

3. *Bed construction of quarter locking wagons such as Surrey, Aylesbury, and West Country.*

4. *Bed construction of most other half locking wagons such as Kent, Sussex, Oxford, Buckinghamshire. It shows the 'keys' on which long boards were laid.*

5. *Skid pan, drug shoe or drug bat for braking a rear wheel.*

6. *Roller scotch, trailed behind a rear wheel when going uphill to prevent wagon running backwards.*

Some carts took peculiar forms as they were designed to meet unusual requirements. One type, known at Great Yarmouth, was used to carry the fish baskets up the beach and through the narrow streets. It was little more than a small platform on wheels, similar to the early wheel car, which were arranged inside the long shafts. This kind of cart was made as narrow as it could possibly be so that it did not obstruct confined alleyways. Another curious vehicle (a dobbin), which was handled by men and not a horse, could once be found in the quarries of Sussex. It had three wheels —one at the front—and was tipped by hand.

There was one interesting, but barbaric, custom associated with carts. Offenders, male or female, found guilty of stealing, vagrancy or other misdemeanours were sometimes sentenced to be whipped at the cart's tail. The victim's wrists were bound to the rear of a cart and he, or she, was led through the streets while an exposed back was flayed with the whip. The last such whipping was probably at Horsham, Sussex, in March 1805 when a man named Feist was "whipped at the cart's tail through the town" for stealing wine. Less fortunate prisoners took their last ride in a cart—to Tyburn gibbet—where Marble Arch now stands.

A Lancashire potato cart

THE WAGON

As far as the Brtish Isles is concerned the wagon seems to have been introduced as late as the sixteenth century by the Dutchmen who came to drain the Fens. For this reason many wagon types which survive in East Anglia retain certain Dutch characteristics—which are outlined in the next chapter. By the late Tudor period communications in England had been improved and lumbering road wagons gradually began to replace pack horses.

A wagon may be divided into two main parts—the under-carriage and the body. There is a common bond to be found in the manner in which traditional wagon underframes were constructed. In contrast, different areas of England produced wagon bodies which differed considerably in design (see the next two chapters). Another odd similarity is the distance between the wheels of wagons and carts, which varied very little throughout the country. The rather arbitrary 4' 8½" track, used as a standard gauge on many of the world's rail-ways, has a very ancient origin. Stephen Dewar has given us a detailed account of "The Oldest Roads in Britain" which may be found around Meare in Somerset—see *The Country-man* Vol. 59 No. 3; Autumn 1962. These ancient tracks radiating from an ancient lake village are made of wooden stakes arranged like the sleepers of a railway track. There is a 'rail' at each side of the trackway—which measures 4' 8" across!—and they are pegged into the peat. Their existence implies the use of wheeled vehicles and advanced archaeolog-ical techniques have demonstrated that these roads also originated in the Neolithic and Bronze Age periods. So, sometimes the width of a wagon's track appears to have a prehistoric origin. This is also true of the structure of a wagon underframe, which has its origins in the European Bronze Age.

The two axles of a wagon are linked together with a coupl-ing pole which is braced to the rear fixed axle. Pole and braces rest immediately upon the axle bed and above them is placed the bolster which supports the body. Many wagons have loose bodies. This allowed the strains of draught to be confined to the undercarriage. Fore wheels have to be smaller to allow for the extra layers of timber required to form the forecarriage—e.g. hounds and the pillow—and to increase the lock by turning further under the body or into a locking arch. The front axle serves two purposes—it must carry part of the weight of the superstructure and permit the

17

forecarriage to turn in a horizontal plane. To prevent the forecarriage from buckling forwards or backwards under the many stresses it undergoes it must be retained in its correct position.

This is achieved by the addition of hounds which are positioned at right angles to the axle bed upon which they rest—at each side of the front end of the coupling pole. The hounds extend furthest to the rear of the axle bed where their extremities are linked by a curved sway bar. As the sway bar passes below and is in contact with the coupling pole the weight of the wagon helps to keep the hounds in a horizontal position. The sway bar and the hounds combine to make an effective lever which determines the precise alignment of the fore axle. This is an ingenious device and its sheer antiquity speaks volumes for the technical skills achieved in an almost forgotten Bronze Age. Above the hounds and coupling pole is bolted another bolster but their combined depth is insufficient to reach the same plane as the rear bolster—so another member is added (a pillow) to provide the body with supports that are in line with one another. The lower face of the pillow and the upper face of the bolster take the friction of the turning forecarriage. Both surfaces are protected by iron plates. The entire structure is linked together by a 1½ inch diameter pin which passes through the pillow, bolster, pole and axle bed to form the pivot about which the forecarriage turns.

Not all wagons have forecarriages that turn the same amount. The degree of turn is limited by the coupling pole, the length of the axle, the size of the wheels and the characteristics of the wagon body itself. Although the undercarriage is a common feature of wagons the details of the bodywork vary considerably. The shape of a wagon body depends upon the kind of frame used to support its floor. Some wagons have a body framework which allows the edge of the wheel to turn into the space provided by the wheel arch.

Other styles of underframe (page 15; 2 and 4) provide a less obvious waist but nevertheless one which will allow the forecarriage to rotate just a few extra degrees. In certain parts of England—Surrey and the western counties—no attempt is made to increase the wagon's lock in this way and vehicles have straight sides (page 15; 3). To increase the lock of a wagon of this kind the axle is lengthened and an appreciable gap is created between the body and the wheels. Slightly waisted and straight sided wagons normally have a small plate attached to the point on the side member where the turning wheel might rub. These plates are known as locking cletes and they provided extra protection for the sides if the chains controlling the amount of rotation did not prevent the fore-carriage from turning too far.

Lock

The amount of turn the forecarriage can achieve is called the 'lock'—a term familiar to motorists. We can distinguish four different kinds of lock—quarter lock, half lock, three quarter lock and full lock. A quarter lock wagon has straight sides and the wheels can only turn as far as the locking cletes on the main side. Wagons with a quarter lock need a wide turning circle as the large forewheels severely limit the angle through which the axle may move. When tractors began to replace horse power on the farm a good many quarter and half lock wagons were dumped under hedgerows to rot. Their limited lock made them unsuitable for conversion to tractor trailers.

Half lock wagons have a waisted body which allows the wheel to turn into the space provided by the wheel arch. They require less space to turn than the quarter lock type.

Wagons with a three quarter lock have smaller forewheels which can turn below the bed of the wagon. The presence of the coupling pole limits the degree of turn and vehicles with this type of lock were not so useful for farmwork, particularly at harvest, as they were far less stable than wagons of the quarter or half lock type. The three quarter lock vehicle was popular with carriers of course as it had considerable advantages on a good road surface.

Fully locking wagons—like those used in Cornwall—had a forecarriage which was not restricted in its movement by a pole. The wheels could move right under the wagon bed until they were at right angles with the rear axle. A full lock wagon had a 'fifth wheel' between the wagon bed and the forecarriage which kept the latter correctly aligned. The fifth wheel is really a strong double iron ring which is fixed to the wagon bed and turning bolster. Major differences in body construction developed from this feature and they were more generally applied to road wagons and the many different kinds of vehicle used in the towns.

When wagons began to be mass produced in factories instead of in the craftsman's shop various short cuts were introduced which enabled a wagon to be made at less cost and in less time. Most factory-made wagons relied a good deal on ironwork for their strength and many were built which did not make use of the traditional coupling pole at all.

The various kinds of vehicle evolved for use in towns had very light bodies and as they were constructed without a pole their wheels were fully locking. Brewers' drays are probably among the best known examples of the many variations of the flat platform wagon. Such vehicles, with shallow sides and canvas covers, were once widely used in towns by the old railway companies for parcel deliveries.

Long boarding, cross boarding

A feature of all wagon bodies is the method of using summers which run parallel with the sides. This arrangement was essential if the weight of the load was to be adequately supported and longitudinal strength maintained.

A wagon fitted with long boards (see page 12) had keys added. The application of a dung cart type of framework to a wagon was not practicable because it would have been far too heavy—even for the huge shire horses. Long boards were not essential for harvest work but various tasks—like carting stones or loose coal—made them essential. The type of floor can sometimes give us a clue to a vehicle's former use and all evidence of this kind needs to be carefully interpreted. George Sturt (*op. cit.*) says that cross boarding was introduced in his part of the country as an economic measure—i.e. it was cheaper than long boards which were laboriously sawn over the pit by hand.

It is not possible to be dogmatic about anything concerned with carts or wagons. Somewhere there will always be an exception to any general rule. Wagon bodies were often built on older undercarriages and the results of such a change can be very misleading to an unwary eye.

Long boarding is not, therefore, always an accurate guide to the age of a wagon. Long boarding persisted in Buckinghamshire until the 1940's but in Norfolk no long boarded wagons have been recorded. In contrast the hoop raved wagons—at least in the South Midlands—appear to have always favoured long boards. There was probably no one universal preference or practice to be found at any time. The type of construction favoured depended upon place, time, cost and local tradition.

Braking

An important feature of any wagon was the method employed to make the vehicle slow down or stop. A number of devices served to assist the wagoner particularly when he was ascending or descending steep hills: dog sticks, roller scotches, skid pans, drug bats and locking chains are all described in the glossary.

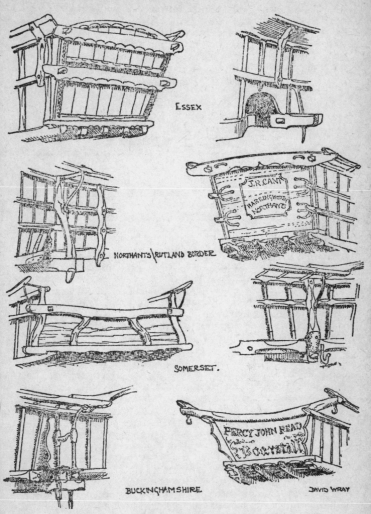

ESSEX

NORTHANTS\RUTLAND BORDER

J.R.CANT
HAREINGWORTH
NORTHANTS

SOMERSET.

BUCKINGHAMSHIRE.

PERCY JOHN READ
BOGYSTALL

DAVID WRAY

*Variety in style - the front boards and waists
of four contrasting wagons.*

21

Painting

The regional preferences for colours is discussed in the next two chapters. Wheels and underframes were almost universally red but the colour used for a wagon body depended upon time, place and the purpose for which the wagon was used. Many wagons still bear the date of the last painting, which is usually found on the tailboard with the painter's name. Great importance was placed upon sending a 'smart' vehicle out on to the road where it met the public gaze.

THE BOX WAGON

The distribution of wagon design across England poses many problems but we can indicate approximate areas of influence and these usually have a close relationship with local geography. Wagons normally co-existed with carts and for many tasks the cart was the superior vehicle.

Lincolnshire

Spindle sided wagons have inherited several characteristics from their Continental ancestors. Apart from the spindle sides the top rail of the Lincolnshire wagon has an attractive curve (see opposite). The body is pitched well above the axles and its high sides—which made it a difficult vehicle to load —help to give it a narrow Dutch look. The spindles in the middle of each side are more or less vertical but those towards the front and rear slope forwards and backwards respectively (see opposite). A single midrail is a characteristic of the Lincolnshire wagon but variations will be found with two midrails. Its body is waisted to allow for a greater lock. The wheels of Lincolnshire wagons tended to be rather large and both broad and narrow tyres were used. The fore and rear wheels are usually about 52 and 60 inches in diameter. Each end of the Lincolnshire wagon was about 6ft. above ground level and this fact alone made it an awkward brute to load. This kind of wagon had a rather high centre of gravity and it gathered a reputation for instability in the vicinity of the Wolds. Two colours were acceptable for the bodywork; red or prussian blue.

Outraves were not used in the north of the county. There, to improve a wagon's capacity, boards with legs that fitted into staples on the top rave were employed. Raves and gormers were fitted at harvest time.

The Lincolnshire wagon could be found in many parts of

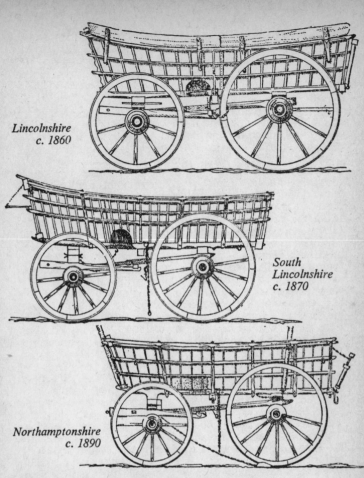

*Lincolnshire
c. 1860*

*South
Lincolnshire
c. 1870*

*Northamptonshire
c. 1890*

*Aylesbury.
Built at
Quainton
c. 1925*

the eastern counties: Kesteven and Lindsey, Leicestershire (The Vale of Belvoir), Nottingham, Rutland and north Norfolk.

Yorkshire

Beyond the Humber the use of wagons was it seems limited to the East and West Ridings. There the style of wagon design took a rather cruder form. Plank sides seem to have been the rule—during the last century at least—and the rather pronounced difference in the size of the fore and rear wheels helps to promote a rather ungainly picture. There is not much to distinguish the Yorkshire style from the mass-produced barge wagons that became so prominent towards the end of the last century. One of the most interesting points to notice about the Yorkshire wagon is the manner in which the fore-carriage provides two inside hounds which project beyond the splinter bar to allow a central pole to be fitted. In the nineteenth century wagons were often drawn by a team of four horses. The front pair were attached to the pole and the rear (wheel) horses were harnessed to whipple trees that were attached to the splinter bar. It is curious to note how long the draught pole idea persisted and it echoes, of course, the days of ox-drawn vehicles. As far south as Sussex oxen were still in regular use until about 1914. The superior speed of the horse gradually made them redundant. It was generally accepted that oxen were more powerful than horses and a record exists of a six-ox team which extracted a wayward 10-ton threshing engine from a pond without any other help. Wagon shafts could be easily changed to allow a pole to be attached. In addition to working a cart or wagon the oxen could be employed on ploughing, harrowing or rolling and they were able to survive on a cheaper diet.

Yorkshire wagons are cross-boarded and the preference for wooden axles, which lasted until the 1880's, helped to maintain the tradition of large naves. Although Yorkshire wagons do not usually vary very much in their design N. A. Huddleston ('Farm Wagons of N.E. Yorkshire'; *Transactions of Yorks. Dialect Soc.*—Vol. LII—1952) has indicated the distinctions which may be made between the relative sizes of the three sub-types he defines. The Dales wagon is the smallest and has a length of some 8 feet. It was mostly used in the north east. The Moors wagon has a length of about 10 feet. This type was to be found in the coastal area north of Scarborough. A third, and largest, variation is known as the Wolds wagon and this vehicle usually has a body length of 12 feet. Size is therefore the principal guide in making a classification of Yorkshire wagons. Brown or red was used for the bodywork and red was the traditional choice for the undercarriage.

Derbyshire

In the area immediately north of Derby another quite distinctive wagon was used which has not previously been recorded in wagon literature. It had very straight spindle sides and two midrails but no outraves. The wagon bed was unusual and possibly unique in that the sides (crooks) were carried right through the shutlock—see page 31. The wheels were normally about 4 inches wide and fitted with hooped tyres. Splinter bars may be found but open hounds are more common. Frontboards bear the owner's name and date—probably of the last painting. Harvest ladders, known as raves and gormers, were used. The bodywork was blue. Its features show that it is more closely related to the Shropshire and Staffordshire wagons than any others.

Essex, Norfolk, Suffolk

The East Anglian wagon has a haughty square appearance. Its sides are panelled and there is one midrail. The curve of the top rail is not so pronounced as the Lincolnshire wagon. In common with all wagon work the body standards are nailed to the planks. Bodywork was usually blue (stone colour also was used in parts of Norfolk) and the underframe red. Another alternative was a white body lined in black. Most wagons in East Anglia were employed for harvest work and their floorboards were placed cross-ways. Where floor boards run parallel with the sides there is an indication that the wagon may have been employed to carry coal or gravel. For work of this kind long boards were helpful in providing a smooth surface for the shovel although cross boarded wagons were sometimes used for this work. Anglian wagons normally have very large rear wheels—up to 6 feet or so—but the fore wheels are relatively small and do not often exceed 4 feet. The massive rear wheels make the body even higher than the Lincolnshire wagons. Harvesters in East Anglia had to hoist their sheaves rather higher than their Lincolnshire neighbours. The forewheels could turn into the waist and the bottom plank was cut away to allow for this improved lock.

One of the most distinctive features of the East Anglian wagon is the interesting way in which the removable frontboard is fixed in position. It oversails the side of the wagon and is held in position by a pin which passes through the projecting siderave—see page 15, w. Not all frontboards were made as tall as the sides, and boards which were as high as the midrail are quite common. Where tailboards were used they fitted over the extended siderave in the same manner.

A curious but rare tradition in East Anglia provided some wagons with forewheels that had a narrower track than the rear wheels. J. G. Jenkins (*op. cit.*) suggests that this usage dates back to the eighteenth century when vehicles which rolled a broad track paid lighter tolls.

The East Anglian wagon usually had twin shafts—such was its laden weight. Its use was widespread in Norfolk and Suffolk but in Essex its distribution was confined to the arable northern portion of the county. Although the vehicle was not used in the Cambridge fenland it could be found in east Cambridgeshire. In Hertfordshire the East Anglian wagon began to rub shoulders with those which show an East Midland influence (see also below—the Hertfordshire wagon).

Hertfordshire

As the influence of the box wagon design filtered westwards into the East Midlands some of its features were modified and adjusted to meet the needs of the Hertfordshire countryside. Many of the surviving wagons which have been recorded come from the end of the last century and they do not always represent the very best examples of craftsmanship. Towards the end of Victoria's reign conditions were poor in certain parts of rural England and economics took precedence over tradition. Another factor which had a definite influence on wagon design was the proximity of London which was expanding its population and its demand for farm produce. A significant part of farm receipts came from London's appetite and, in addition to the farm wagon, we must not overlook the vast numbers of road wagons which daily made their way to London. The differences between the road wagon and a farm wagon are sometimes rather subtle but in general terms the former did not need to be quite so robust. At harvest time no doubt a good many road wagons would also be seen in the fields.

The typical Hertfordshire wagon is cross boarded, has iron spindle sides and two midrails. There are usually five strouters supporting the sides—from which spring two outraves. Most Hertfordshire wagons are rather shorter in length than those found in East Anglia or in the Rutland area and they do not often exceed 10 feet—although some longer specimens will be encountered. The design of the frontboard varied—some were only as high as the midrail but there were large numbers of wagons with frontboards as high as the sides. Wheels tended to be rather narrow and most were not more than 3

Norfolk c. 1840

Norfolk
'Factory' wagon
c. 1920

Suffolk
c. 1880

Probably Cam-
bridgeshire. Barge
wagon body on
old bed and
undercarriage.

inches in width. This feature too helped to add to the impression of lightness conveyed by the Hertfordshire pattern. Brown was the usual colour for the farm wagon with buff for the undercarriage. Road wagons, which had to give a good impression, seem to have favoured blue for the body with the usual red below. Towards the end of the last century the introduction of springs on road wagons, and carts, began to have an effect on village workshops. It seems probable that the products of London factories played some part in influencing developments in the Home Counties. The use of springs and the decline in the quality of the ironwork are among the more obvious effects to be noted. Until late in the reign of Victoria the Hertfordshire village wheelwrights produced their own versions of the accepted local wagon design, but not far away a variation on the Hertfordshire theme was also established.

Buckinghamshire

Buckinghamshire is often considered to be hoop-raved wagon territory but it produced an interesting box wagon that has not previously attracted much attention. The Aylesbury Hybrid represents an adaptation of the Hertfordshire design. Its spindle sided body has one midrail which is pitched slightly above the centre. Like the Hertfordshire pattern the top rail is level but it is supported by up to six strouters. There is one outrave. In common with other wagons of this kind the forehead projects to provide support for the raves. An interesting mannerism associated with the Aylesbury wagon is the way the sideboards are scalloped at their edges between the spindles. Farm and road wagons alike were treated in this way. The wagon bed is cross boarded with wide elm boards—not deal. Splinter bars are commonly found and dog sticks are almost always fitted. Front and rear ladders are used. The wagon sides are deep and nearly vertical. Front boards bear the name and address of the owner. Yellow was often used—like the Woodstock wagon—but blue was frequently employed particularly for road wagons. A deep scarlet was used for the wheels and undercarriage.

Later versions of this style may be found without a pole but with a very light body and a fully locking fore-carriage. These less robust specimens were road wagons and iron spindles occur in place of timber. The quality of the ironwork, which was very similar to the Oxford style, also declined and the embellishments employed by the blacksmiths of earlier years disappeared—twists and involutes gave way to plain curves. It seems likely that the hybrid design was not mass produced in a factory because it appears to be confined to a rather small area—mid-Bucks and the Hertfordshire border. There were certainly enough wheelwrights at work to account for their distribution and the variations in detail.

In the Chilterns there was once a miniature type of box wagon that served a very special purpose—collecting flints for roadmaking. The flints came mostly from the ploughings and the farmer was not sorry to lose them—for the ploughman's sake. Women and children were employed on stone picking but children were particularly useful as their wages were a pittance. The absence of a child from school for even a prolonged period was not unusual—a girl of nine years was once absent for 15 weeks "picking stones in the fields". This Chiltern wagon was about 8 feet in length and 3 feet wide. The smaller wheelbase limited the size of the wheels and the body was therefore low pitched. As children provided the backbone of the labour force one can appreciate the need for a vehicle of smaller dimensions than the traditional wagon. A wagon of ordinary dimensions would have been an impossible vehicle to deal with on the steep slopes of the Chilterns if it was laden with stones. The Chiltern wagon has iron spindle sides and two deep boards which are separated by a single midrail. There is a narrow lade supported by three iron brackets. Wooden strouters added to the strength of the sides which were of usual box wagon proportions but nevertheless rather low. A slender name board was fixed to the right hand side. The top rail was straight. Frontboards equalled the sides in depth and the vehicle generally echoed the characteristics of the Aylesbury Hybrid described above. Both types of wagon probably date from the second half of the last century. The Chiltern wagon can claim distinction by usage and size.

Northamptonshire, Bedfordshire, Huntingdonshire, Rutland, Leicestershire, Warwickshire

The Northamptonshire wagon has a wide area of influence and will also be found in Bedfordshire, parts of Cambridgeshire, Huntingdonshire, Rutland, Leicestershire and Warwickshire. Local traditions will frequently modify detail but throughout this area the general characteristics of the Northampton pattern persist. Towards the north and east the vehicles tend to become larger and heavier.

In common with the other East Anglian wagons the Rutland wagon retains the preference for two midrails and spindle sides. Unlike the Hertfordshire type it has a high curving front board which is an elegant and distinctive feature. The mid-raves are fixed to the frontboard by means of elaborately forged strap bolts. These often have the appearance of ancient iron hinges seen on church doors. Usually the bolt is fashioned in a trident shape but all kinds of variations occur. The owner's name is placed among flourishes within an oval on the frontboard. There is a very unusual tailboard on wagons of this type. It is made so that it can be used as a ladder for climbing into the back of the wagon. Some were fitted with harvest poles.

Earlier versions may have straight frames but waisted frames became fashionable after the 1850's and both may still be found. Wooden strouters, not so elegantly curved as the Hertfordshire kind, provide the foundation for the iron brackets which support the outrave. In profile the side dips very gently towards the middle. The forewheels are usually about a foot smaller than those at the rear.

In northern Northamptonshire and Rutland a brilliant orange was used all over. Other colours used were red, blue and (in Bedfordshire) brown.

Herefordshire, Worcestershire, Monmouthshire

We can distinguish two kinds of box wagons in this part of England. The traditional Herefordshire wagon has panel sides and two midrails which project beyond the frontboard. To echo this embellishment the side planks are also carved and they extend forwards beyond the frontboard. This gives the forward end a decorative, toothed look which is characteristic. The heavy wheels are up to 7 inches wide and there are two rows of strake tyres. Both pairs of wheels are quite large —about 4 feet and 5 feet respectively—and the lock was therefore limited. These wagons are rather heavy vehicles and a pair of horses were often employed. The body—about 12 feet long—has long boards.

Thomas Hennell—*Change in the Farm*—sketched the late nineteenth century alternative to the panel sided wagon. Its successor has plank sides but the general heaviness remains. An interesting survival can be observed on these plank sided wagons. Two incised lines replace the midrails and remind us of their antiquity. The front end is swept upwards to allow the heavy straked wheels a little more lock. Robust strouters are fashioned in a double curve, but the ironwork begins to have a spidery look. Another detail of interest the artist recorded was the use of harvest poles like those used in Kent— see front cover. The Herefordshire plank sided wagon illustrates very clearly the manner in which the traditional panel sided design was gradually discarded in favour of the less

*Derbyshire
by Bond, near
Mackworth c. 1890*

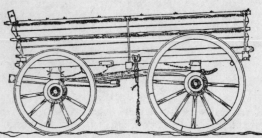

*Derbyshire.
Barge wagon
c. 1910-1920*

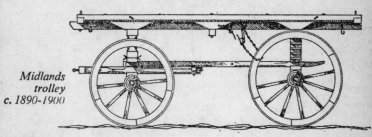

*Midlands
trolley
c. 1890-1900*

*Warwickshire
1912*

expensive and mass produced alternative. Wagons of this type did not have outraves and Thomas Hennell's drawing shows how harvest ladders were sometimes permanently fixed in position with iron brackets.

The Worcestershire wagon is very similar in construction and its plank sides, which retain the double groove to show where the midrails once were, are divided by rectangular standards. An outrave, which is heavily scalloped, is supported by rather plain iron brackets which are fixed to the standards. The features described place this type of wagon in the last quarter of the nineteenth century.

The Monmouthshire style of wagon was similar to the Worcestershire but it lacked the refinements. Perhaps it is for this reason that it appears to be rather heavier and somewhat crudely made. A Monmouthshire wagon can be seen at the Museum of English Rural Life, Reading. This specimen, derived from Tirley, Glos., is rather interesting. The donor was W. R. Fowler and three members of the same family—J. P. Fowler, John Fowler and Guy Fowler—were farming in the same village in 1914. It seems likely that this wagon was made in the workshops of the Sparrow brothers —the village wheelwrights. At the time of the First World War there were still over 170 wheelwrights to be found in Gloucestershire and this gives some indication of the extent of horse drawn transport at that time.

Radnorshire

The countryside around the southern border of Wales is rich in apple orchards which produce the raw material for the cider makers. From Radnorshire we inherit a wagon which was not intended to carry hay or corn at all. Its structure is designed to bear dense burdens, including apples, and the principal strouter is U-shaped. The wagon sides are panelled and the flat sectioned standards are divided by a single midrail. The 3 inch wide wheels of a Radnor wagon are much narrower than the Herefordshire, and hooped tyres are used instead of strakes. Twin shafts are fixed to the splinter bar on the forecarriage. In contrast to the Monmouth wagon the front end of the Radnor vehicle has a definite upward sweep. The frontboard is arched and the forehead projects at each side.

Shropshire, Montgomeryshire

The Shropshire wagon has panelled sides, its standards are flat in the Monmouthshire style, and there is a single midrail. Towards the ends the wagon sides are curved upwards and in profile the body is concave. An interesting feature on the body is the universal use of wooden strouters and brackets to support the outrave. In a county which is renowned for iron-working pioneers it is rather paradoxical to note how the conservative wheelwrights resisted the introduction of a new material. Even in the area around Coalbrookdale itself wagons were made in this century with completely wooden axles. Wheels with a pronounced dish were always wide—about 6 inches—and fitted with strakes. Yellow was the standard colour and no additional decoration was used.

Most of the Montgomeryshire wagons date from the last quarter of the nineteenth century and they have several points of similarity with the heavier Shropshire design. The main difference to note is the omission of a midrail—standards are present and slender iron brackets spring from them to support the outrave. Plank sides project beyond the frontboard and they help to suggest the barge wagon shape. In Montgomery wheels are usually narrower—about 3 inches—but strakes are still employed. From the relative lightness of the design it is easy to see that the Montgomery version was a cheaper alternative to its more robust Shropshire cousin.

Denbighshire, Flint

The style of wagon found in the northern parts of Wales has some interesting comparisons with those so far described. One characteristic distinction is the way in which the wagon body is made to be higher at the rear so that both frame and floor have a forward slope. Although the top rail is straight the wagon has a sloping profile. Denbighshire wagons are not principally harvest vehicles and they are made to handle heavy and dense loads. The framework is therefore particularly large. Panelled sides and two midrails add to the strength of the body which is supported by wide curving strouters. These provide an anchorage for the sturdy iron brackets which hold the outrave. Body standards slope forward or backward according to their positions. The frontboard, which has the same features as the sides, rises in an arch above the top rave. Hoop tyres (3 inches wide) and strakes (6 inches wide) may be found on wagons of this type. The bodywork is finished in red and/or blue.

Staffordshire

The wagons of the Staffordshire design—which probably spread out into parts of Leicestershire, Warwickshire, Shropshire and Cheshire—are particularly heavy. A large panel-sided body with a single deep midrail has an almost flat profile. The standards—about 14—are closer together and consequently more numerous than on most box wagons. Lades are wide and flat. One reason for the heaviness of the style is the exceptional dimensions of the straked wheels which can be as much as 8 inches wide. Hooped wheels are about half as wide but they are still relatively heavy. Equally robust naves have a cone-shaped exterior. Up to six horses were sometimes required to pull these very heavy vehicles which could be over 12 feet in length. Blue is the usual colour for the body but yellow will be found towards the west.

Sussex

The south-eastern corner of England is still box wagon country but the geography and the size of farm holdings combined to make its vehicles lighter in construction than those found north of the Thames. Sussex wagons are half-locking and both spindle and panel sided examples will be found with one midrail. Panels tended to predominate in the east of the county and spindle sides in the north and west; nearer Surrey, poles were more commonly used than ladders at harvest time—as in Kent. So that a harvest load could be securely tied rope rollers were fitted under the shutlock. Open hounds on the fore-carriage are the general rule and wooden axles may still be found.

Sussex wagons often have a loose body which is secured at the rear by a bolt passing through the end of the pole and a wooden bar which is bolted to the summers in front of the shutlock. The loose body idea is widespread in this corner of England and its influence has no doubt had an effect on the development of wagon design. It is suggested that wagons in this corner of the country owe much to the timber wagons that must have been predominant hereabouts in the days when England was defended by her "wooden walls" constructed in the shipyards at Deptford, Chatham, Sheerness, Portsmouth, Plymouth and Beaulieu. In those days, as the timber close to the coast was gradually consumed, longer treks were made for oak which took the wagons up into the Weald. We have the evidence—provided by John Constable—of the famous *Haywain* to show us that timber wagons were also employed for agricultural purposes.

Not all wagons were made with loose bodies of course and certain fixed-body wagons were constructed without pole braces. Shaped blocks of wood were attached to the ends of their axle beds to support the bolster—see page 13. The Sussex road wagons were frequently cross-boarded and the boards of some were left loose. This was to allow gravel or road metal to be discharged through the bed instead of being heaved out at the back or over the sides. Hoop tyres

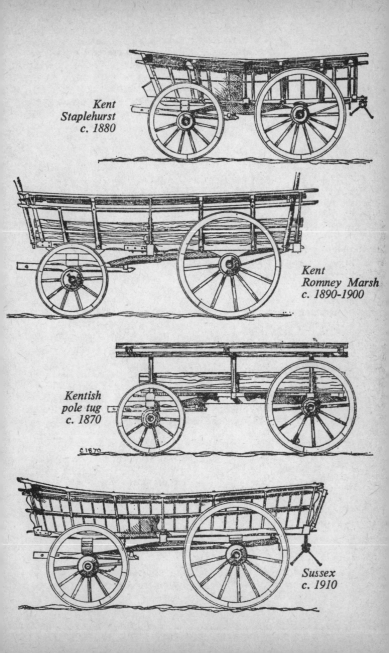

*Kent
Staplehurst
c. 1880*

*Kent
Romney Marsh
c. 1890-1900*

*Kentish
pole tug
c. 1870*

*Sussex
c. 1910*

or strakes (for 6 inch wheels) and wooden axles will be encountered. There are usually four strouters at each side fashioned in a double curve. Blue is the usual colour for the bodywork.

In the extreme east of the county the Kent wagon is dominant—see below. The term 'Sussex wagon' has often been wrongly applied to the Kent design. The fascinating working drawing published by the Science Museum is labelled Sussex simply because it portrays the type of wagon made at Northiam.

Kent

The Kent wagon—see cover—is one of the most attractive box wagons. It is distinguished from all other wagons by the manner in which the undercarriage is arranged. The pole is bolted directly to the central summer of the wagon bed and there are no pole braces. Kentish wagons are half lock vehicles and hoop tyres are far more common than strakes. The wagon body is panelled. Provision is made for harvest poles at each corner. Buff is the usual colour for wagons but blue seems to have been favoured for carts and sometimes also for wagons. Wheels and the undercarriage were finished in red.

Another interesting wagon may be found in Kent. It is known as a pole tug or bavin tug. Bavin is the Kentish word for a bundle of brushwood and the principal task performed by the pole tug was to carry the bundles of hop poles to the fields. The pole tug—page 35—has a traditional kind of underframe with pole and braces. Upright stifers (standards) are mortised into the top rave and the front and rear bolsters. This arrangement on some wagons provides a framework for plank sides which are nailed into position. The bed, if floored, has long boards. There are no front or tailboards. Wagons of this kind—with rough sides and floor—could be used for various tasks. One such wagon, which had a front axle inherited from a stage coach, was used in the latter years of Victoria's reign for transporting stone. These wagons, with their harvest poles, could be seen at work with the Kentish wagons at harvest time.

In the hopfields a miniature wagon—called an alley bodger —was used for collecting the hops. It could be drawn from either end by a horse hitched to staples by means of chain traces, and had four small iron wheels on fixed axles.

Surrey

The Surrey wagon—so well documented by George Sturt, *op. cit.*—was not confined strictly to the county and its use

*Dorset
Bridport area
c. 1860*

Dorset c. 1890-1910

Sussex c. 1870-80

*Surrey
Farnham
c. 1860*

spilled over into parts of Sussex, Hampshire and even Berkshire. Spindle sides are general and there is a single midrail. Surrey wagons have distinctive and beautifully shaped wooden strouters which sit in equally elegant iron sockets—which are also to be found in Sussex and to the west. Unlike Sussex or Kent the body is not waisted and the side timbers are more or less straight—they do in fact have an upward curve towards the front end. Hoop tyres came into use late in the last century as George Sturt describes. Various colours may be used for the body—brown, buff or blue. As the county has become increasingly urbanized examples of the Surrey wagon have become hardest to find.

Dorset

One of the smallest English box wagons will be found in Dorset. The body is not often much more than 10 feet in length and the rather wide track of the wheels gives it a wide appearance. Some wagons are nearly square in plan! Dorset wagons are particularly strong as two or three extra crossledges, of smaller size than the main crossledge, are added to the bed. A similar feature will be noted on the wagons of Wiltshire, Somerset, Devon and S.W. Gloucestershire. It is a common practice in the western counties to end crossledges flush with the side and to cover the ends with a strouter. The top rail is curved gracefully and, at the front, the concave top rail (the forehead) of the frontboard oversails the sides to provide a support for the outraves. Wheels have hooped tyres. Rear wheels can be as small as 4 feet and tyres a mere 2 inches wide. Yellow or blue was employed for the bodywork. Dorset wagons were also used in the neighbouring counties to the west and in parts of Hampshire.

All wagons varied in detail and, depending upon the time, place of origin and the requirements of the buyer, tradition slowly diverged to meet the demands of economics. In this way the box wagon was gradually replaced by the boat wagon that was usually, but not always, the product of the factory.

THE HOOP-RAVED WAGON

The most elegant of all English wagons is the style built with a hooped rave that curled upwards above the hind wheels. It is surprising how much difference this feature makes to the look of a wagon—see page 41. Wagons of this kind were extensively employed in the South Midland area and to the south and west. The wheelwrights in this region encountered design problems that did not concern builders of box wagons. Apart from the detailed differences of spindle or panel sides various ways were evolved to make a top rave start from the forehead in the usual way and curve upwards over the hind wheel before descending to meet the tailboard. A hooped rave wagon is basically a box wagon with a raised curving side over the hind wheels.

If we accept the theory that the Dutchmen probably added the wagon to English transport we may wonder how such a different kind of wagon body could have been evolved. What were the reasons for altering the box shaped body that served half of England so well? There is probably not a single simple answer to this question and it seems that the design was slowly worked out over a long period of time. A painting of Salisbury Cathedral by John Constable—who must have known the details of East Anglian wagons very well, suggests that the hooped rave idea was in use and fairly well advanced by the end of the eighteenth century—see below. In the Cotswolds, Chilterns, and on the Wiltshire downland there are many arguments in favour of a wagon with a good carrying capacity and sides that are not too high. The hooped rave certainly added to the wagon's capacity and the idea seems to have worked its way up from the remote Cornish peninsula. Spindle sides are often found on wagons of the kind and we can probably explain their use partly as an inheritance from the kind of construction used on mediaeval carts.

Buckinghamshire and Oxfordshire

The body of the South Midland hoop-raved wagon is very shallow. Spindles decorate and strengthen its waisted sides. Where the rear wheel rises above the top rave a hooped rave is added to make the foundation of the wheel arch. The forehead of the plain frontboard is concave and it spreads out its chamfered horns beyond the sides where it gives support to the outrave. This is attached to the sides by spindles set into drilled holes on the upper rave. The outrave is sometimes straight but more often curved in a concave fashion until it meets the rolling rave that soars up above the rear wheel. There are usually four iron brackets for support—at the waist, above the axles and at the rear. These are common features on all hoop-raved wagons. In Oxfordshire and Buckinghamshire the older wagons have brackets which are shaped like an H if viewed from the side. An alternative design—like a letter N—has much simpler lines and is probably a later variation. Most wagons were long-boarded. Front ladders were always carried, and in the Cotswolds harvest poles were used. Tailboards are either solid or made with open spindles set in a straight bottom and convex top rail. Chains fixed to the sides allowed the tailboard to be set at any desired angle —thus fulfilling the function of a rear ladder. These were not often fitted but their use was widespread in the area around the Vale of Aylesbury. The rear wheels are usually about five feet in diameter. Strakes and hoops will be found on wagons of this kind. Wheels vary considerably in width from 2½ to as much as 8 inches. The bodywork is usually yellow and wheels are red. In Buckinghamshire the ironwork is black but in the Cotswolds blue was used. The under- carriage is often more elaborately chamfered than on any other kind of wagon—but this embellishment is never carried to the point of excess.

Wagons of this type were first described as early as 1809 when Arthur Young made a detailed drawing of one. He called it a 'Woodstock wagon' and this name has been attached to it ever since—an alternative is 'Oxford wagon'. A few years before, in 1789, Marshall in his *Rural Economy of Gloucestershire* had noted it as being "the best farm wagon in the Kingdom" and commended its efficiency and ability to carry high loads without overturning. Among all English wagons the Woodstock wagon alone can claim supreme elegance. From Young's time until the dawn of the present century the basic design of the Woodstock remained unchanged and the high standards of craftsmanship endured. Unlike East Anglia there was no debased form of the trad- itional style of vehicle.

In parts of Oxfordshire a smaller version of the Woodstock was built. It was in fact a half locking box wagon as its sides were straight and there was no hooped rave. All other details were in the Oxford tradition, however, and it there- fore justifies an acknowledgement here.

Wiltshire and West Berkshire

The wagons of Wiltshire and West Berkshire conformed to the general hooped-rave pattern. A characteristic feature was the way in which the outrave swept down to join the hind shutlock that was extended beyond the sides. The boarded lades do not have the accomplished sweep of the Woodstock wagon. James Arnold, *op. cit.*, points out that one variant around Devizes lacked a hooped rave altogether as the sides were deeper and cleared the rear wheel—see page 45. There is a difference between the bodywork in these two counties. Wiltshire wagons have straight sides and Berkshire

40

Somerset

West Gloucestershire

Wiltshire

Oxfordshire c. 1860

wagons are half-locking. The sides are normally panelled in place of the Oxford spindles. The bed of the Wiltshire wagon has extra cross-ledges, like those already noted in Dorset above. Few Wiltshire wagons will be found with long boards which seem to have gone out of favour in the 1870-80 period. Hooped tyres and strakes were used and the width of the wheels varied from about 3 to 6 inches. The West Berkshire style represents a fusion of ideas borrowed from Wiltshire and Oxford. Wiltshire used blue for the bodywork but the Berkshire preference was yellow. Wagons that have been 'done up' of course do not always appear in traditional or original colours. Names of owners usually appeared on the frontboard and the painter or wheelwright often added his name at the rear. The date of building or repainting was also recorded.

Hampshire

The style of hoop-raved wagon found in north-west Hampshire had a strong affinity with the Berkshire and Wiltshire wagons mentioned above. Like the Berkshire style it had a half-locking bed. The sideboards had two intermediate rails instead of boards. High curving ladders were used at front and rear. Wagons usually had blue bodies. Hampshire is an in-between area where box and hooped rave wagons may be found; it came under the influence of several adjacent counties —e.g. Surrey and Dorset.

Dorset

Ideas were often borrowed from other counties as has already been shown. Dorset was no exception and the county's hoop-raved wagon shares certain characteristics with the Dorset box wagon already described. It has straight sides with flat standards divided by a single midrail. The wooden strouters, the four summers, and the peculiar construction of the forecarriage with its third central hound, are all borrowed from the west. Iron brackets support a flat lade and the hoop rave itself is joined to the shutlock. These wagons have an ungainly appearance and they are relatively rare. On the western fringes of Hampshire, wagons of this kind were called 'Somerset wagons' and we can therefore add this misnomer to our list. Blue was the usual colour for the bodywork.

Gloucestershire and North Somerset

The hoop-raved wagons found here were mostly used west of the Cotswold scarp. They have the shallowest of all bodies and their curves, which are so carefully wrought, have an unquestionable beauty. Thomas Hennel's *Change in the Farm* drawing of one at West Littleton is worth special study. Broad wheels with a double line of strakes—a usage dictated by the soil—are relatively common. Examples will be found with a complete iron axle extending from side to side, in place of the usual axle arm. Axles of this kind are sometimes strengthened by a form of wooden axle bed—a feature also found in West Wiltshire. Blue is the usual colour for the body.

A wagon has been noted (at Chipping Sodbury) without a coupling pole. Two braces were scarfed together at the front and extended to the forecarriage where the turning pin passed through them. They therefore served a dual purpose.

Somerset and Devon

Although the Somerset wagons are rather larger than their Devon neighbours the characteristics of both are very similar. In shape they are quite distinctive as the hoop-rave continues in a horizontal plane rearwards of the wheel. Wagons of this kind are sometimes known as cock-raved—from an alleged similarity between the rear end which sticks up like a cockerel's tail. They are also known locally as ship-wagons, as their rear end is not unlike a ship's poop deck. The wagon bed narrows at the crossledge but it is not waisted. To improve the lock the sides rise sharply above the forewheels. Crossboards usually rest on the four summers. Panel and spindle sided examples may be encountered. Ironwork is frequently sparse, particularly in Devon, and wooden brackets and strouters are set in sockets nailed to the sides. Light iron brackets support the outraves. Iron spindles link the top rave and the two outer raves together. These wagons have an attractive appearance which derives from their proportions and the chamfering of slats and strouters. The frontboards oversail the lades and the top rail and middle rail butt up against the back of the forehead and frontboard. Both are secured with strap bolts. If iron middle and hind staffs are used they are often elaborately twisted and their lower ends sometimes have a ring which fits round the end of the shut-lock. Head and tail ladders are used.

Devon wagons favoured a dark blue with a pinkish red. Somerset used a lighter blue or even yellow. Chamfering, which was often stepped, or painted to give this impression, was picked out in contrasting colours: red on yellow or blue, black on red. The front and tail boards were painted with similar care. The owner's name was shown on the front amid suitable flourishes and the builder placed his on the rear. Small wheels, about 4′ 6″ on average at the rear and 3′ 4″/

3′ 8″ at the front, help to make the wagon closer to the ground and therefore easier to load. Square tongued spokes are normal on these wheels, which seldom exceed four inches in width. Both strakes and hoops were used. Hubs often have a dirt ring spiked onto their inner ends which helped to keep mud off the axle arm.

On certain late wagons the cock-rave was omitted, which made them box wagons but with the local features already described. Wagons of this kind often had a fake midrail which was half-lapped over the body standards.

Cornwall

Cornwall was really cart country but a light form of wagon was used where the terrain allowed. Cornish wagons are a four wheeled version of the jack-wain (page 7). Cornwall is credited with the introduction of the first fully locking wagons and as their hind wheels rose above the bed a hoop-rave was constructed to protect the wheel. David Wray thinks that here we see the true origin of the hoop-raved wagon. The idea could have worked its way up from Cornwall and gradually attached itself to the various kinds of box wagon that it met on its way. It is perhaps not without significance that the hoop-raved idea was brought to a pinnacle of fulfilment around the Midland counties—where perhaps it met an inherited tradition for the box shape which was in turn derived from Dutch influences once present in the Fens.

In south-east Cornwall wagons with very low, splayed out sides—in the boat wagon tradition—may be seen. These are also fully locking.

Glamorganshire

The Gloucestershire type of hoop-raved wagon (see page 41) had an influence beyond the Severn and it was widely used in Glamorgan during the nineteenth century. On later versions the hooped rave became a plain lade. Wheels were straked or hooped. The colour for the bodywork was also inherited from Gloucestershire.

Convictions concerning the relative merits of box or hoop-raved wagons and their numerous variations will depend upon sentiment and the reader's place and date of birth. Wagons viewed in childhood have a universal habit of diminishing in size with the passage of time! Those who saw shocks standing golden in the sun, heard creaking sides straining with a load, smelt horse and felt stubbles tremble under a measured tread will know that a laden wagon has the majesty of a ship under sail.

*North Cornwall
c. 1890*

*South
Cornwall
c. 1910*

Devon 1863

South West Wiltshire c. 1900

BOAT AND BARGE WAGONS

Two types of wagon still need to be considered. Both emerged, in the nineteenth century, as distinctive variations on older themes. Boat and barge wagons usually retain the traditional undercarriage but later examples even dispensed with this feature. Each represents the gradual changes which overtook traditional methods and materials. These changes were inspired, of course, principally by economic considerations.

Boat wagons usually have a three-quarter lock. Their side-boards, often made with two planks, slope outwards like a boat's hull. The angle between the lower and upper board is sometimes almost 180° (a straight line) and the upper board then serves as the lade. These wagons became very popular alternatives to the traditional hoop-raved wagons. Both could be seen working in the same village. It seems as if the credit for inventing the boat shape belongs to Taskers of Andover in Hampshire. The design seems to have been widely copied and different versions and sizes of boat wagons may be encountered. Village wheelwrights also produced boat wagons and the design was not solely the product of factories.

Barge wagons may be distinguished from the older box wagon style by the manner in which the body is made. The method of fixing the plank sides to barge wagons was simple and depended upon a series of long bolts which passed through raves, planks and side timbers. In effect the whole side was clamped together in the vice-like grip of the bolts. An advantage of this kind of construction was the amount of labour it saved and this helped to make the finished product cheaper. We can therefore see how the traditional box wagon design began to degenerate under economic pressures. The barge wagon, which showed an increasing reliance on iron-work epitomizes this decline. As the pressures of national economic life slowly permeated the countryside so the village wheelwright too had to accept the need to build cheaper vehicles. Many barge wagons were probably made by village craftsmen although the majority came from factories where mass production was the rule.

Boat and barge wagons often have iron wheel centres in place of elm naves. The use of cast iron for wheels dates from at least 1846 when a set of 'Prize Patent Wheels and Axle' which could carry 30 cwt. was offered in an advertisement for £6 10s. 0d.

Typical three quarter lock boat wagon c. 1900

Devon Buckrowe 1892

West Midlands barge wagon

Barge wagon by Crosskills, Beverley, Yorks. c. 1910

PLACES TO VISIT

This list is of places where carts and wagons are on display. Where appropriate the hours of opening are given, but before making a special visit to a distant museum the reader is advised to check the current arrangements. A ready source of reference for this kind of information is *Museums and Galleries in Great Britain and Ireland* which is published annually by ABC Travel Guides Ltd.—most libraries have copies.

AVON
Bristol City Museum
Queen's Road, Bristol 8 (Tel. Bristol 27256).
Open: weekdays 10—5.30.

BERKSHIRE
Reading University Museum of English Rural Life
Whiteknights Park, Reading (Tel. Reading 85123).
Open: Tues—Sat., 10—1 and 2—4.30. An appointment must be made with the Keeper to see the forty vehicles in this collection, for they are not on display.

BUCKINGHAMSHIRE
Stacey Hill Collection
Wolverton.
Open: Bank Holidays in summer, and other times as advertised locally.

DEVON
Arlington Court (N.T.)
near Barnstaple (Tel. Shirwell 296).
Open: April to mid-October, 11—1 and 2—6.

Bicton Countryside Museum
Bicton Gardens, East Budleigh (Tel. East Budleigh 2820).
Open: Easter to Spring Bank Holiday and mid-September to mid-October, daily 2—6; Spring Bank Holiday to mid-September, daily 10—6.

Buckland Abbey (N.T.)
near Plymouth (Tel. Yelverton 3607).
Open: Good Friday to September, weekdays 11—6, Sun 2—6; October to Good Friday, Wed., Sat. and Sun. 3—5.

DURHAM
North of England Open Air Museum
Beamish Hall, Beamish (Tel. Stanley 3586).
Open: Easter to September, Tues. to Sun. and Bank Holiday
Mon. 10—5 (till 9 on Wed. in summer); October to March,
Tues. to Sun. and Bank Holidays 1—4.

EAST SUSSEX
Michelham Priory
near Hailsham.
Open: Easter to October, 11—5.30.

ESSEX
The Barn Restaurant
Braintree (Tel. Braintree 656).
Exhibits in the open—visitors always welcome.

GLOUCESTERSHIRE
Snowshill Manor (N.T.)
near Broadway (Tel. Broadway 2410).
Open: May to September, Wed. Thurs., Sat., Sun. and Bank
Holiday Mon., 11—1 and 2—6; April and October, Sat., Sun.
and Bank Holiday Mon., 11—1 and 2—6 (or dusk if earlier).

HAMPSHIRE
County Council Collection
Chilcombe House, Bar End, Winchester.
It is hoped to establish a Museum of Hampshire Rural Life
here.

KENT
Wye College Agricultural Museum
Court Lodge Farm, Brook, Wye (Tel. Wye 401).
Open: June to September, Wed. 2—5 (also Sat. in August),
and by appointment with Curator.

LEICESTERSHIRE
Leicester Museum of Technology
Abbey Pumping Station, Corporation Road, Leicester.
Open: weekdays (except Tues.) 10—5, Sun. 2—5.

Rutland County Museum
Catmos Street, Oakham (Tel. Oakham 3654).
Open: October to April, weekdays (except Mon.) 10—12,
2—4; May to September, weekdays (except Mon.) 10—12,
2—5; Sun. 2—5.

LINCOLNSHIRE
Museum of Lincolnshire Life
Lincolnshire Association, County Centre, Burton Road, Lincoln (Tel. Lincoln 29864).
Open: daily (except Mon.) 2—5.

NORFOLK
Bridewell Museum of Local Industries & Rural Crafts
Bridewell Alley, Norwich (Tel. Norwich 22233).
Open: weekdays 10—5.

NORTH YORKSHIRE
Ryedale Folk Museum
Hutton-le-Hole (Tel. Lastingham 367).
Open: Easter to September, daily (except Tues. and Fri. in April and May) 2—6 (11—6 mid-July and August).

York Castle Museum
Tower Street, York (Tel. York 53611).
Open: April to September, weekdays 9.30—7.30, Sun. 10—7.30; October to March, weekdays 9.30—4.30.

OXFORDSHIRE
Oxford City and County Museum
Fletcher's House, Woodstock (Tel. Woodstock 811456).
Open: May to September, Mon. to Fri. 10—5, Sat. 10—6, Sun. 2—6; October to April, weekdays 10—5.

SALOP
White House Country Life Museum
Aston Munslow.
Open: April to October, Sat. 11—6 and Wed. 2—6; also July to mid-September, Mon., Wed. and Thurs. 2—6; Good Friday 2—6; Bank Holiday weeks (except Fri. and Sun.) 11—6.

STAFFORDSHIRE
Staffordshire County Museum and Mansion House
Shugborough, Stafford (Tel. Little Haywood 388).
Open: mid-March to mid-October, weekdays (except Mon.) 11—5.30, Sun. and Bank Holidays 2—5.30.

SUFFOLK
Easton Farm Park
Model Farm, Easton, Woodbridge (Tel. Wickham Market 74657).
Open: early April to mid-October, Wed. to Sun. 10.30—6.

Museum of East Anglian Life.
Stowmarket (Tel. Stowmarket 2229).
Open: April to October, 2—5.

WARWICKSHIRE
Mary Arden's House
Wilmcote, Stratford-upon-Avon (Tel. Stratford-upon-Avon 4016).
Open: April to October, weekdays 9—6, Sun. 2—6; November to March, weekdays 9—12.45, 2—4.

WEST SUSSEX
Horsham Museum
Causeway House, Horsham.
Open: Tues. to Sat. 1—4.

WEST YORKSHIRE
Tolson Memorial Museum
Ravensknowle Park, Wakefield Road, Huddersfield (Tel. Huddersfield 30591).
Open: weekdays 10.30—5, Sun. 2—5.

West Yorkshire Folk Museum
Shibden Hall, Shibden Park, Halifax (Tel. Halifax 52246).
Open: April to September, weekdays 11—7, Sun. 2—5; October and March, weekdays 11—5, Sun. 2—5; February, Sun. 2—5.

WILTSHIRE
George Inn
Sandy Lane, Chippenham (Tel. Bromham 403).

WORCESTERSHIRE
Avoncroft Museum of Buildings
Stoke Heath, Bromsgrove (Tel. Bromsgrove 31886).
Open: end of March to end of October, 11—6 daily except Mondays, but open Bank Holiday Mondays.

Worcestershire County Museum
Hartlebury Castle, near Kidderminster (Tel. Hartlebury 416).
Open: February to November, Mon. to Thurs. 10—6, Sat. and Sun. 2—6.

WALES
Welsh Folk Museum
St. Fagans Castle, St. Fagans (Tel. Cardiff 561357).
Open: April to September, weekdays 10—7, Sun. 2.30—7; October to March, weekdays 10—5, Sun. 2.30—5.

GLOSSARY

Arm: the iron or wooden spindle upon which the wheel turns.

Axle bed: the wooden beam to which the axle arm is fixed.

Axle tree: an all wood axle with wooden arms.

Box: the hardened metal centre of the nave—which runs on the axle.

Braces: a pair of timbers attached to the pole to keep it at right angles to the rear axle.

Chamfer: the decoration resulting from the shaving of timbers in order to reduce the vehicle's weight.

Collet: a washer on the axle arm to protect the lynch pin.

Copse: an iron stay keeping the outrave in position.

Crook: the curved separate section of the sides of a waisted wagon.

Crossledge: the central cross member of a wagon body. It may be curved and deep with crooks mortised into it or light, straight and bolted to crooks/summers. The ends usually project ten inches beyond the sides to support the middle stave which buttresses the side.

Dirt iron: metal plate projecting from the axle bed to protect the space between it and the stock.

Dish: name given to the concave arrangement of the spokes. See Sturt *op. cit.*

Dog stick: wooden stick fixed to an axle tree. It has a forked metal end. Going uphill it was allowed to drag on the ground. If the vehicle stopped the stick was pushed into the surface and prevented the wagon running backwards.

Draught pin: a metal pin used to fix shafts to hounds or splinter bar.

Drayel: a form of long staple attached to the front end of shafts—for a trace horse.

Drug bat: a cast iron wedge-shaped shoe which was placed under a hind wheel when going downhill so that it would 'skid' and lessen the wagon's speed. The wear was taken by the wedge and not the tyre.

Ex bed: a common name for the axle bed.

Felloe: a section of a wheel's rim.

Fifth wheel: flat rings of iron usually about two feet in diameter which are fixed to the turning pillar and bolster of a fore carriage to maintain its vertical alignment.

Forehead: the upper part of the front end of a wagon/cart body.

Hermaphrodite: a curious vehicle (found in East Anglia,

Lincs., Notts., etc.) which is half cart and half wagon. Used in the late eighteenth century. It is basically a cart body with an added forecarriage. The carrying capacity is increased by the addition of a flat platform which rests on the head of the cart and is supported by standards resting on the pillow/bolster above the forecarriage.

Hound: part of the forecarriage framework. See page 15; 1, k.

Keys: timbers placed at right angles to the summers to provide fixing points for long boards.

Ladder: the framework used to extend the carrying capacity of the wagon or cart.

Lades: the overhanging shelf projecting from the top rave of the sideboards to increase the carrying capacity and prevent the load fouling the wheels.

Locking arch: the cavity formed in the bed of a half locking wagon to allow the forewheels the maximum turning space —e.g. Lincolnshire and East Anglian wagons.

Locking chain: a long and short length of chain fixed to a wagon or cart side to lock a wheel and prevent it turning. The short end has a ring and dog hook. The long end is passed around the felloes and clipped to the dog. These chains are normally fixed to the nearside—sometimes on both.

Locking cletes: iron plates fixed to the sides to protect them at the point where the forewheels meet the body when turning.

Long boards: boards running parallel with the wagon/cart sides. Opposite to cross boards which were fixed directly to the summers.

Long staple: a fitting on upper side of shafts. There are usually three hooks on the offside and two hooks plus a ridgetie on the other. The front hooks are for the draught chains fixed to the horse's collar. The rear hooks take the breeching chains. The centre hook on the offside is for the free end of the ridgetie which passes over the pad/saddle and supports the weight of the shafts.

Lynch pin: the pin at the end of the axle arm which keeps the wheel in place.

Nave: the elm hub into which the spokes are mortised.

Nosepiece: the front crosspiece of a cart/wagon bed.

Outrave: the rail, held in place by the copses, which overhangs the sides of a cart/wagon.

Panel sides: a term often loosely employed to describe slats or standards nailed to the side planks. These give the impression of panelling but there is no such thing as a "panelled" wagon.

Pole: the long coupling pole which joins the forecarriage to the rear.

Propstick: a short stick hung below the shafts of a cart. When the cart was at rest it was allowed to drop down and take the weight off the horse's back.

Rail: cross members on head/tail boards; the upper rail on a frontboard is also called the forehead.

Rave: usually any longitudinal timber on or attached to the sides.

Roller chain: a chain for the roller scotch.

Roller scotch: a cylindrical piece of wood which rolled along just behind the rear wheel when going uphill. If the wagon stopped and began to run backwards the rearward motion was 'scotched'—hence the saying.

Shutlock: the end cross members of a cart/wagon body.

Shutter: cross timbers joining a pair of shafts, hounds or the mainsides of a dung cart.

Sides: the outer lower timbers of a cart/wagon bed. See Crook.

Skid pan: an alternative name for a drug bat.

Slider, sway bar: a slightly curved timber connecting the rear end of the hounds. Usually faced with metal on the upper surface which bears against the underside of the pole. It prevents the forecarriage from folding up under the wagon.

Spindle sides: wooden or iron spindles used to strengthen the body sides.

Splinter bar: the cross piece on the forecarriage to which the shafts are fixed.

Staff, stave: forged iron brackets buttressing the sideboard against the weight of a load which tends to push wagon/cart sides outwards.

Standards: the slats fixed to the body planks to resemble panels.

Stock: same as nave.

Stock bond: iron rings shrunk on to a stock/nave, in front and behind the spokes, to prevent splitting.

Stopper: the wooden block closing the slot cut in the face of the stock to allow the lynch pin to be withdrawn.

Stopper clasp: an iron catch shaped like a flattened cabinet hook to keep the stopper in place. Very occasionally a short chain is used instead.

Strake: an iron tyre made in sections and nailed to the wheel.

Strouter: a wooden support to strengthen the wagon side; often worked into elegant curves with the spokeshave.

Summer: part of the body framework of a wagon/cart which is parallel to the sides and joined to the shutlocks.

Tip stick: a device for controlling the degree of tip on a cart body.

Traveller: a disc on a handle used by the blacksmith for measuring the circumference of wheels and tyres.

Tumbril: an ancient name for a cart, used latterly in East Anglia.

BIBLIOGRAPHY

ARNOLD, JAMES—*The Farm Waggons of England and Wales* John Baker 1969. An attractive and informative book presented in a landscape format. There is a good illustrated introduction which is followed by twenty-four of James Arnold's splendid coloured plates. It is a pity the relevant text does not face them. The author's extensive researches have enabled him to provide a fascinating chart showing how much the names for a wagon's component parts differ in the ten counties quoted. A limited edition of 1800 each signed by the author.

BAILEY, JOCELYN—*The Village Wheelwright and Carpenter* Shire 1975. Illustrated paperback.

EVANS, GEORGE EWART—*The Horse in the Furrow* Faber 1960. This is essential reading for those who want to know more about the related subject of horse-lore. An outstanding book with excellent drawings by C. F. Tunnicliffe.

JENKINS, J. GERAINT—*The English Farm Wagon* Oakwood Press for the University of Reading 1961. Illustrated with plates and drawings. There is a useful appendix which records detailed measurements of the specific wagon types defined.

STURT, GEORGE (George Bourne)—*The Wheelwright's Shop* Cambridge University Press; first published 1923, paperback edn. 1963. A classic in its field which describes a Surrey wheelwright's way of life in the closing years of the last century. Here the reader will find the making of a wagon explained in detail and catch a glimpse of the skills that started with the selection of the standing timber itself.

VINCE, JOHN—*Farms and Farming* Ian Allan 1971.

WRIGHT, PHILIP A.—*Old Farm Implements* David & Charles. Includes illustrations of wagons and tumbrils.